Gone!
Stegosaurus

Rupert Matthews

www.heinemann.co.uk/library
Visit our website to find out more information about Heinemann Library books.

To order:

Phone ++44 (0)1865 888066
Send a fax to ++44 (0)1865 314091
Visit the Heinemann Bookshop at www.heinemann.co.uk/library to browse our catalogue and order online.

First published in Great Britain by Heinemann Library, Halley Court, Jordan Hill, Oxford OX2 8EJ, a part of Harcourt Education. Heinemann is a registered trademark of Harcourt Education Ltd.

Editorial: Andrew Farrow and Dan Nunn
Design: Ron Kamen and Paul Davies and Associates
Illustrations: James Field of Simon Girling and Associates
Picture Research: Rebecca Sodergren and Ginny Stroud-Lewis
Production: Viv Hichens
Originated by Ambassador Litho Ltd
Printed and bound in China by South China Printing Company

07 06 05 04 03   08 07 06 05 04
10 9 8 7 6 5 4 3 2 1   10 9 8 7 6 5 4 3 2 1
ISBN 0 431 16614 5   ISBN 0 431 16619 6
(hardback)   (paperback)

British Library Cataloguing in Publication Data
Matthews, Rupert
Stegosaurus. - (Gone forever)
1. Stegosaurus - Juvenile literature
I. Title
567.9'153

Acknowledgements
The Publishers are grateful to the following for permission to reproduce copyright material: Corbis pp. 16 (Paul A. Souders), 24 (Richard Cummins); Geoscience Features pp. 6, 8, 12, 14, 18, 20, 22; Natural History Museum, London pp. 4, 10; Senekenberg Nature Museum/DK p. 26.

Cover photo reproduced with permission of Geoscience Features.

Our thanks to Dr Angela Milner of the Natural History Museum, London for her assistance in the preparation of this book.

Every effort has been made to contact copyright holders of any material reproduced in this book. Any omissions will be rectified in subsequent printings if notice is given to the Publishers.

Disclaimer

All the Internet addresses (URLs) given in this book were valid at the time of going to press. However, due to the dynamic nature of the Internet, some addresses may have changed, or sites may have ceased to exist since publication. While the author and Publishers regret any inconvenience this may cause readers, no responsibility for any such changes can be accepted by either the author or the Publishers.

Contents

Some words are shown in bold, **like this**.
You can find out what they mean by looking in the Glossary.

Gone forever!

Sometimes all the animals of a particular type die. This means the animal has become **extinct**. Scientists called **palaeontologists** study the **fossils** of these animals. The scientists find out about the animal and how it lived.

Stegosaurus

Brachiosaurus

The **dinosaur** called Stegosaurus is an extinct animal. It lived about 150 million years ago in North America. It ate plants. All the other dinosaurs that lived at this time have also become extinct.

5

Home of Stegosaurus

Geologists are scientists who study rocks. They have looked at the rocks where **fossils** of Stegosaurus have been found. These rocks can tell us many things about the place where Stegosaurus lived.

Stegosaurus lived in a wide, flat land. Huge rivers flowed across the land. The weather was warm and often damp. There were areas of wet **marsh**, but trees grew on the drier land.

Green and brown

The rocks that contain **fossils** of Stegosaurus also contain the fossils of plants. Fir trees, **monkey-puzzle** trees and **gingko** trees all grew at the time of Stegosaurus. Similar plants still grow today.

fossil of leaves from a gingko tree

cycadeoid   gingko   pine tree

horsetail   fern

There were many more **ferns** and **horsetails** at the time of Stegosaurus than today. They grew much larger than the ones alive now. There were also plants that are now **extinct**. One of these was the **cycadeoid**. The cycadeoid had a short, fat trunk and a clump of leaves like fern leaves.

In the shadow of Stegosaurus

Scientists have also found **fossils** of small animals in the same rocks as Stegosaurus. This shows that they lived at the same time as Stegosaurus. One of these fossils was a frog. It looked similar to the fossil frog shown here.

fossil of a frog —

There were many other small animals living alongside Stegosaurus. There were **insects**, **newts** and **lizards**. There were also **mammals** that looked like **shrews**. These hunted insects.

cockroach

shrew-like mammal

lizard

frog

newt

What was Stegosaurus?

Scientists who study **fossils** can tell what an animal looked like and how it lived. These **palaeontologists** have studied the fossils of Stegosaurus. They know it was a **dinosaur** that ate plants.

head

tail

Palaeontologists know that Stegosaurus was about seven to nine metres long. Stegosaurus had a very small head. It had a brain the size of a walnut, even though its body was larger than a car. It was probably not very clever!

Baby Stegosaurus

Scientists have found **fossils** of **dinosaur** eggs. However, no eggs belonging to Stegosaurus have been found. Perhaps Stegosaurus partly buried its eggs in the ground, like these eggs below.

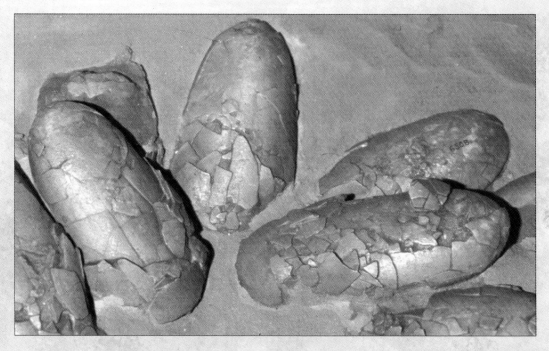

fossils of eggs belonging to Oviraptor

No evidence of baby Stegosaurus has been found. When the eggs **hatched**, perhaps Stegosaurus babies dug their way out of the ground. Then they might have hidden in thick undergrowth. There they would have been safer from attack.

Reaching for food

The front legs of Stegosaurus were much shorter than the back legs. This means that the head was held close to the ground. Stegosaurus could crouch down so that its head could reach right down to the ground.

Scientists think Stegosaurus ate plants that grew no taller than about one metre. The most common plants of that size were **ferns**. Scientists think Stegosaurus probably ate ferns.

Stegosaurus dinner

The **fossils** of Stegosaurus show that it had small teeth. Its jaws were also small. They had only weak **muscles** to make them work. This meant that Stegosaurus could not chew tough plants very well.

Stegosaurus jaws

Scientists think that Stegosaurus bit off pieces of **fern**. It swallowed them without chewing. The ferns were **digested** in the stomach for a long time. This meant that Stegosaurus needed to have a huge stomach.

Clash of rivals

Stegosaurus had large upright plates along its back. These were made of bone covered with skin. Scientists think that Stegosaurus might have been able to change the colour of its skin. This would have looked very dramatic.

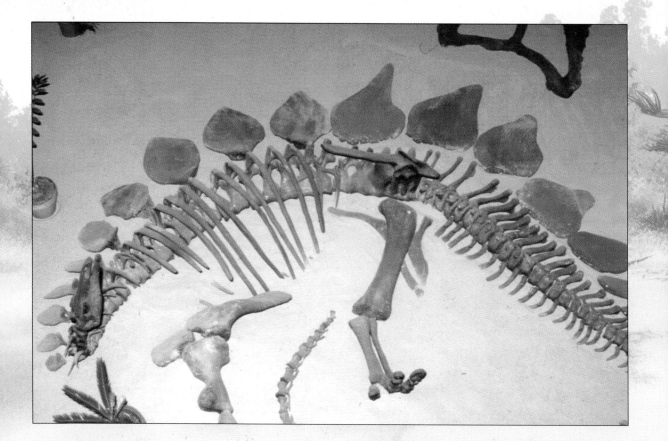

Sometimes two Stegosaurus would want to feed in the same area. Perhaps the **dinosaurs** used their plates and changed colour to make themselves look scary and powerful. The one that made the best display would scare the other Stegosaurus away.

Keeping warm

The **fossils** of plates on the back of Stegosaurus are covered with grooves and ridges. These grooves show that Stegosaurus had many **blood vessels** that carried blood over the plates.

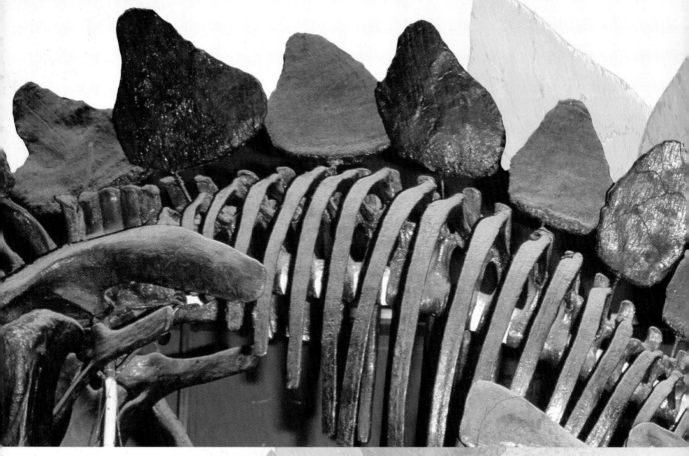

Some scientists think that Stegosaurus used the plates to control its temperature. Perhaps it used them to warm up by catching the sunlight. Or maybe it used them to cool down, like the ears of a modern elephant.

Under threat!

Scientists know that a **dinosaur** called Allosaurus lived at the same time as Stegosaurus. Allosaurus was a large **predator**. It would have hunted Stegosaurus for food.

Scientists think Allosaurus might have hidden among trees. It would dash out to attack any Stegosaurus that came close. Allosaurus could kill Stegosaurus using its long claws and sharp teeth.

Fighting back

Stegosaurus **fossils** show that it had four large spikes on the end of its tail. These spikes were made of bone and were very sharp.

Scientists think that Stegosaurus could use the spikes to defend itself. Stegosaurus would lash its tail from side to side. Allosaurus would not want to be injured. This might make it leave Stegosaurus alone.

Stegosaurus around the world

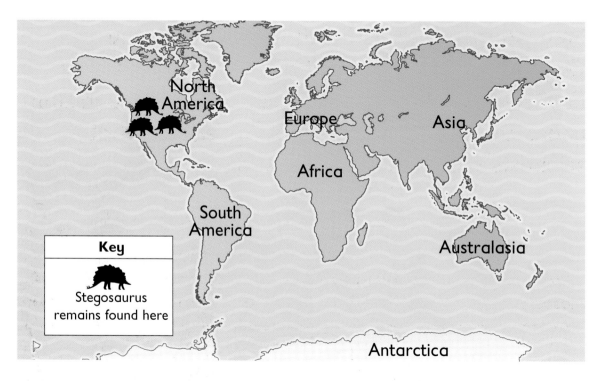

The **fossils** of Stegosaurus have been found in several parts of North America. The fossils of similar animals have been found in Africa, China and Europe.

When did Stegosaurus live?

Stegosaurus lived on Earth in the Age of the **Dinosaurs**. Scientists call this time the Mesozoic Era. Stegosaurus lived between 150 and 140 million years ago (mya). This was at the end of what scientists call the Jurassic Period.

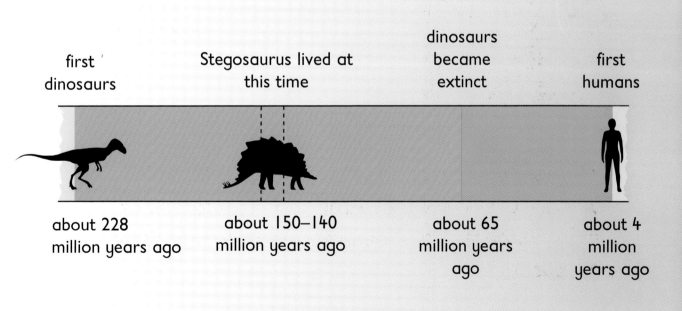

first dinosaurs	Stegosaurus lived at this time	dinosaurs became extinct	first humans
about 228 million years ago	about 150–140 million years ago	about 65 million years ago	about 4 million years ago

Fact file

Stegosaurus fact file	
Length:	up to 9 metres
Height:	up to 5 metres
Weight:	about 2 tonnes
Time:	Late Jurassic Period, about 150–140 million years ago
Place:	North America

How to say it

Allosaurus – al-oh-saw-rus   dinosaur – dine-oh-saw
cycadeoid – sigh-kad-ee-oid   Stegosaurus – stegg-oh-saw-rus

Glossary

blood vessels tubes carrying blood around the body

cycadeoids plants that looked like a cross between a palm and a fern, but that were unrelated to both. They are now extinct.

digested food that has been broken down so it can be used by the body

dinosaurs reptiles that lived on Earth between 228 and 65 million years ago. Dinosaurs are extinct.

extinct an animal is extinct when there are none left alive

fern green plant with large feathery leaves and no flowers

fossils remains of a plant or animal, usually found in rocks

geologist scientist who studies rocks

gingko type of tree with fan-shaped leaves

hatch when a baby dinosaur breaks out of its egg

horsetail type of plant with an upright stem and spiky leaves

insect small creature with a hard outer covering and six legs

lizard small reptile with four legs

mammal animal with hair or fur. Mammals give birth to live young instead of laying eggs. They also feed their young on milk.

marsh land that is partly covered by water

monkey-puzzle type of tree with spiked branches

muscles parts of an animal's body that provide power to make it move

newt small animal with four legs that lives in and out of water

palaeontologist scientist who studies fossils. Palaeontologists discover things about extinct animals, such as dinosaurs.

predator animal that hunts other animals, which it then eats as food

shrew type of small mammal with a long nose

Find out more

These are some other books about dinosaurs:

Stegosaurus and Other Jurassic Plant-eaters, Daniel Cohen
(Capstone Press, 1996)
Big Book of Dinosaurs, Angela Wilkes (Dorling Kindersley, 2001)
Dinosaur Park, Nick Denchfield (Macmillan, 1998)

Look at these websites for more information:

www.enchantedlearning.com/subjects/dinosaur/dinos/
www.oink.demon.co.uk/topics/dinosaur.htm
www.stegosaurus.org/

Index